SUMMARY

of

Mastering Diabetes

*The Revolutionary Method to Reverse
Insulin Resistance Permanently in
Type 1, Type 1.5, Type 2, Prediabetes,
and Gestational Diabetes*

by

Cyrus Khambatta, Ph.D.

& Robby Barbaro, MPH

BOOK TIGERS

Note to readers:

This is an unofficial summary & analysis of Mastering Diabetes: The Revolutionary Method to Reverse Insulin Resistance Permanently in Type 1, Type 1.5, Type 2, Prediabetes, and Gestational Diabetes by Cyrus Khambatta, Ph.D. and Robby Barbaro, MPH, designed to enrich your reading experience.

Scan here to buy the original book.

approved, licensed, or endorsed by the aforementioned interests or any of their licensees.

The information in this book has been provided for educational and entertainment purposes only.

The information contained in this book has been compiled from sources deemed reliable and it is accurate to the best of the Author's knowledge; however, the Author cannot guarantee its accuracy and validity and cannot be held liable for any errors or omissions. Upon using the information contained in this book, you agree to hold harmless the author from and against any damages, costs, and expenses, including any legal fees, potentially resulting from the application of any of the information provided by this guide. The disclaimer applies to any damages or injury caused by the use and application, whether directly or indirectly, of any advice or information presented, whether for breach of contract, tort, neglect, personal injury, criminal intent, or under any other cause of action. You agree to accept all risks of using the information presented inside this book.

The fact that an individual or organization is referred to in this document as a citation or source of information does not imply that the author or publisher endorses the information that the individual or organization provided. This is an unofficial summary & analytical review and has not been approved by the original author of the book.

Download Your Free Gift

Before you go any further, why not pick up a free gift from me to you?

Natural Detox Strategies

Discover The Most Effective Detox Strategies For a Successful Cleanse.

Scan the barcode to get it before it expires!

Table of Contents

Summary Overview

The book Mastering Diabetes focuses on the underlying cause of diabetes, some of the science behind it and offers an alternative lifestyle to treat it. The first part of the book aims at a deeper understanding of insulin resistance. It discusses how animal and processed foods affect the body and explains why the conventional low-carbohydrate, high-fat, high protein diet is wrong. It offers an alternative low-fat plant-based whole-food lifestyle that promises to reverse insulin resistance on all types of diabetes and eradicate every common complication of diabetes. The second part of the book is a step-by-step process of building a lifestyle full of habits that utilize a proper diet, fasting and exercising to guarantee an energetic, satisfying, delicious, colorful and athletic everyday life. It teaches how to transition safely from the conventional diet to the Mastering Diabetes lifestyle, how to adapt medication, how to start changing each meal of the day to follow this revolutionary method and offers a system that leaves no room for hunger. The book offers more than 30 delicious recipes and gives excellent cooking advice to prepare food that maintains its nutrients. The effects of the Mastering Diabetes method are no less than extraordinary.

Chapter By Chapter Analysis

The Mastering Diabetes method that was developed by Cyrus Khabatta Ph.D. and Robby Barbaro MPH is presented and examined thoroughly in their new book with the same title "Mastering Diabetes: The Revolutionary Method to Reverse Insulin Resistance Permanently in Type 1, Type 1.5, Type 2, Prediabetes, and Gestational Diabetes". The foreword of the book is written by Neal Barnard, MD President of the Physicians Committee for Responsible Medicine who reminds the reader how diabetes is considered and treated as a lifelong condition, but with the method described in this book, people can master diabetes or even get rid of it. He talks about how observations in countries that changed their diet inspired the method and how their team put their new ideas to the test with the support of the National Institutes of Health and the collaboration of Yale University. This book puts the power to master diabetes to the reader himself.

Chapter 1

The first chapter of the books consists of four distinct parts and is titled "This Book Can Save Your Life". The first part with the title of the chapter "This Book Can Save Your Life" starts by stating the staggering amount of $327 billion that diabetes as a pandemic cost in 2017 to the United States. Millions of people suffer from various types of diabetes, cost 2.3 times more in medical expenses and are dramatically more vulnerable to an extensive list of chronic diseases like cancer and Alzheimer's disease. The authors promise to teach a way to completely reverse prediabetes and non-insulin-dependent type 2 diabetes while maximizing insulin sensitivity, reducing the overall need for basal and bolus insulin, and offering higher control to blood glucose for anyone suffering from type 1, type 1.5 diabetes or insulin-dependent type 2 diabetes. Their method is counterintuitive, challenges the traditional ways of treating diabetes, and offers a holistic and everyday applicable approach to the condition. It is so effective that "A Note to the Reader" interrupts the first part of the chapter to suggest working closely with a physician, personal monitoring of blood glucose, and quick adjustment of oral medication to prevent dangerous situations. The Mastering Diabetes Coaching Program, the authors' online program that this book is derived from, is unique, daily tested and provides repeatable results like dropping A1c levels to 5.6%, reducing by 10-60% both basal and bolus insulin use, weight loss, improvement of digestive functions and an overall health betterment.

The second part of chapter one "A New Approach to Understanding – and Mastering – Diabetes" refers to the authors' own experience with diabetes; they were both diagnosed early in their life with type 1 diabetes. Following the popular medically orthodox low-carbohydrate, high-fat, high-protein diet the author's physical and emotional health declined rapidly, like so many others before them, and led to their decision to question the conventional way. Each author followed his own path, experimented with different diets but ended up in the same conclusion: "A low-fat plant-based whole-food lifestyle is the most effective way to gain insulin sensitivity using your food as medicine." They figured out that carbohydrate-rich whole foods require large amounts of insulin if and only if the total amount of fat in your diet is also high, radically changed their diet, and together developed the Mastering Diabetes method. The method encompasses four components. The first component "Low-Fat Plant-Based Whole-Food Nutrition" encourages the consumption of carbohydrate-rich foods and includes all the scientific rationale that supports it.

"Intermittent Fasting", the second component, offers fasting routines and practices that among others improve insulin sensitivity and offer increased lifespan. The third component "Daily Movement" highlights the importance of physical activity and teaches the most appropriate ways of combining exercise with the rest of the method's practices. Lastly, the "Decision Trees" component is a tool that simplifies and guides the complicated, everyday decisions of diabetes patients and explains the level of disorders of glucose. Furthermore, the Mastering Diabetes coaching program plugs the participant in a community that can support and encourage him in his new path. This part of the chapter ends with some testimonials of people who have followed this method. Then the third part "How Many Types of Diabetes Are There?" defines and describes the causes of all types of diabetes. The final part of the chapter bears the title "The Mastering Diabetes Method" and emphasizes the importance of daily habits to anyone's health and concludes that healthy habits are what this book will attempt to develop.

Chapter 2

Chapter two is titled "The Mastering Diabetes Approach" and starts by describing briefly the structure of the book and its step-by-step approach. In the beginning, Tami's story- a client of the authors and a participant of their coaching program- is told focused on her medical details and her extraordinary improvement to underline the effectiveness of the program. Then the reader is introduced to the five-step approach. The first step is explaining the roots and exploring what is insulin resistance and how it's affected by food. The goal is a long term success through understanding and careful planning. The authors have categorized food in three categories, green light, yellow light, and red light foods which respectively improve insulin sensitivity should be eaten only occasionally, and create insulin resistance. Common questions and problems are also addressed like rapid loss weight or how to transit to a plant-based diet. The second step is all about meals and changing one meal at a time. Starting at breakfast with a shift from high-fat, high-protein to high-carbohydrate foods, continuing with lunch, and how to make a calorie-dense plant-based meal, while finishing with dinner and planning a vegetable centered meal with fruits and mushrooms. In the third step, the book will attempt to carefully integrate some intermittent fasting techniques to reap its benefits. Exercising regularly and choosing the reader's favorite routine is the fourth step. The final step, the latter part of the book, discusses strategies that will help sustain this healthy lifestyle in tricky situations.

The rest of the chapter recounts the story of the authors since their diagnose with type 1 diabetes and the various ways they coped with it. Just before that part, they emphasize- through a brief part titled "One Size Fits… No One"- the importance of customizing the method to each individual's preferences, career, and people in their life. Cyrus Khambatta was diagnosed at the age of 22 with insulin-dependent type 1 diabetes, making it his third autoimmune condition in six months. Frightened he tried to control his blood glucose by adjusting his diet, exercising, and taking insulin. He followed his doctors' advice for nine months, but at a "moment of pure frustration" and blood glucose three times higher than it should have been, he decided to take matters into his own hands. He turned to a more plant-based diet and from mechanical engineering, he started studying biochemistry and ended up earning a Ph.D. in nutritional biochemistry. He's taken the mission since to educate people with diabetes and transform their lives from the inside out. Robby Barbaro was diagnosed younger, at the age of 12, with type 1 diabetes, but chooses every day to see it as an "inconvenience". As a type-A personality, he researched heavily about his diet, experimented widely, but he still suffered from allergies, plantar fasciitis, and cystic acne. He went from drinking awful tea to a ketogenic diet but encountered various problems. When he was introduced to the work of Douglas Graham, DC, his life changed, he read about Cyrus's story, he participated in the coaching program and even started a nonprofit organization. He's since created the

Mastering Diabetes program, earned a master's degree in public health, freed himself from his other conditions, and since dedicated to this mission. The chapter ends with an encouragement to look at diabetes as part of ourselves and not a monster to be "conquered".

Chapter 3

"What Really Causes Insulin Resistance?" is the title of chapter three and starts with another brief success story of the author's coaching program. In the beginning, the chapter deconstructs and points out the mistakes of the conventional carbohydrate-centric diabetes model - doctors can't be blamed, they aren't educated in nutrition. "The carbohydrate-centric diabetes model argues that carbohydrates turn into sugar, which then spikes your blood glucose and triggers the production of large amounts of insulin. As a result, your muscle, liver, and adipose tissue become resistant to insulin, in an effort to protect themselves against excess insulin." The underline assumption is that carbohydrates spike blood glucose if and only if the baseline level of insulin resistance is high, to begin with. The four mistakes of this model are underscored. Firstly the community fails to describe the fundamental difference between natural sugars (monosaccharides) and manmade, refined sugars; secondly the belief that insulin is a terrible hormone, when in fact excess insulin is the problem. Thirdly failing again to distinct between "carbs" of processed foods and whole foods and lastly, studies on "low-fat" diets are poorly designed.

The next part of the chapter explains the role of insulin and is sub-headed "Human Biology 101". Insulin works as an escort for glucose and informs the cells that glucose is available in the blood to import. Glucose is fuel for cells. The liver, muscles, and brain account for the majority of glucose absorption in the body, which makes insulin essential for life. Cells can only absorb glucose if and only if they have the ability to recognize insulin's presence. If they can't, then glucose gets trapped in the blood, while the pancreas releases more insulin to compensate. Insulin resistance occurs when cells constantly reject insulin, which happens for many reasons. Dominant among them is diet, meaning the amount, the type and the macronutrient ratio (the ratio of carbohydrates to fat to protein) consumed. Carbohydrates aren't dangerous; instead, fatty acids directly inhibit the action of insulin. Fat and carbohydrates are mutually exclusive fuels and a high-fat diet induces insulin resistance by the accumulation of excess fat in tissues that are not designed for that.

"A Step-by-Step Overview of the Fat-Insulin Connection" analyzes in six steps that exact relation. On step one, the process of fat entering the bloodstream before glucose is explained, where fat is absorbed into the lymphatic system and the stomach is signaled to slow down digesting. Thus carbohydrate and protein digestion stay behind. Next, fat is transferred in the form of chylomicron particles into the liver, which "repackages" them to lipoproteins and releases them in the blood. Since fatty acids and cholesterol don't need insulin to enter cells as lipoproteins, they are immediately burned for energy and stored away. Unfortunately, cells are not equipped to block excess fat from entering and being stored. On step three, fat enters the adipose tissue, which is an alternate fat storage facility, works as a protective organ, and only increases the risk for chronic diseases when excess fat is stored. Cells in the adipose tissue can swell and break when chronically overfed, recruiting macrophages to clean up the cellular debris and triggering a low-grade inflammation that reduces the ability of insulin to function properly, the fourth step explains. The fifth step describes the process in which "Fat Causes Insulin Rejection in Your Muscle and Liver". Since fatty acids are available sooner and in bigger quantities during digestion, the liver and muscle cells alter their internal composition to digest fat and block out glucose by rejecting insulin. That results in excess insulin, ineffective communication with the liver, and surplus glucose in the blood. The sixth and final step discusses beta cells, which are the only cells capable of secreting insulin, but when they are overworked, they commit suicide; and since their death is largely irreversible, the body's insulin needs are hard to satisfy, unless they are reduced by a proper lifestyle. The chapter ends by highlighting that insulin resistance can affect anyone and is different from autoimmune diabetes.

Chapter 4

In chapter 4 the authors declare that "All fat is not created equal" starting with Lindsay's story to point out that not only the quantity but also the quality of consumed fat is very important. They divide the chapter into three major parts to talk about each kind of fatty acid. Specifically, "Trans Fatty Acids", naturally occurring in small quantities in beef, pork, lamb, butter, and milk, are exceedingly present on processed foods and are produced by the hydrogenation process. Seemingly safer than cholesterol, they actually cause more metabolic damage and are associated with an increasing list of cardiovascular and cognitive decline conditions. The second kind, "Saturated Fatty Acids" that are found in whole foods, animal and dairy products are a more controversial issue on whether they improve diabetes patients' health. Although diets rich in saturated fat help decrease blood glucose and weight in the short term, they significantly increase insulin resistance in numerous ways. They impose danger for liver diseases and elevate the levels of LDL cholesterol, a known and powerful risk factor for coronary and heart diseases. In a short box titled "Cholesterol 101", the book gets into details about cholesterol and concludes the part proposing to lower the intake of saturated fat considerably.

On the contrary, "Unsaturated Fatty Acids", the third and last part of the chapter, are the least harmful type of fat, synthesized endogenously (monounsaturated fatty acids/MUFA's) or dietary taken (polyunsaturated fatty acids/PUFA's) from fish, vegetables and seeds. Especially PUFA's are associated with increased insulin sensitivity and thus reduced diabetes risk, decreased LDL levels, and cardiovascular risk. Nevertheless, the authors advise that seeds, vegetables and other foods rich in PUFA's should be consumed in small quantities, since all whole foods contain fat, in order to avoid larger fat intake than expected and boost insulin resistance. The Mastering Diabetes Method takes all of this into account when constructing meals.

Chapter 5

The next chapter titled "Contributing Culprits: Animal Foods" starts with the extraordinary story of one of the current coaches of the Mastering Diabetes team to underscore the impact of a change from a meat-based to a plant-based diet can have. In the debate of whether meat and dairy products develop insulin resistance and diabetes, the authors refer to specific studies in this part of the book to highlight the correlation between high animal food intake and chronic disease risk titling the section "What Large-Scale Studies have to say about it". Reviewing 5 such studies and one meta-analysis they point towards the undeniably strong and positive association between meat consumption of any kind, and diabetes risk. They summarize the results in an easy-to-read table. Next, the book answers the question "Are Eggs Safe to Eat?" by listing numerous studies and their results on the correlation of egg consumption and long-term diseases, which is significantly positive and recommend reducing or even eliminating them altogether.

The following part discusses some metabolites that meat and dairy products contain. The first is leucine, an amino acid that puts tissues in a prolonged high-energy state that causes many problems, like eventual beta-cell suicide. Next is heme iron, a mineral mostly found in animals, which under normal doses is useful and essential, but in even little excess raises the risk for diabetes outstandingly. Nitrates are naturally occurring compounds on certain vegetables and pose no threat when consumed from those sources. But when added in meat along with nitrites pose a serious long-term danger and the presence of heme iron aggravate the effect. Added sodium in processed meat also raises the risk of diabetes and is found from a large-scale study to be the strongest predictor of type 2 diabetes. Finally, a diverse collection of compounds called advanced glycation end products (AGEs) can be found in foods cooked in low-moisture environments or can be formed in the body when sugar combines with lipids or amino acids. They are linked with many diabetes complications.

The next part is titled "How Meat and Dairy Affect Your Risk for Autoimmune Diabetes" and answers the question of whether there are certain foods that increase the risk for autoimmune diabetes. There is a specific pathogen called MAP (mycobacterium avium paratuberculosis) that using the process molecular mimicry tricks the human body and eventually makes it destroy its own beta cells resulting in near or complete loss of insulin production. MAP infects animals and especially industrialized cows and through the production process directly contaminates all products.

A strong argument is also made about the different effects proteins from different sources have. Animal sources contain proteins that promote mortality, but plant-based proteins have a protective effect according to a study mentioned. Concerning fish, there isn't consistent research linking them to increased diabetes risk; however, they are contaminated through processes like bioaccumulation with numerous environmental pollutants, like mercury, dioxins, and PCBs that are harmful to the human body. For any nutrients the consumption of fish provides, the authors propose alternate sources and minimizing fish intake.

Chapter 6

"Your Carbohydrate Master Class" is the title of the sixth chapter and gets into details about the metabolic effects of carbohydrates. Similarly, like every chapter, it begins with a triumph of the Mastering Diabetes Method giving numbers and details. The book tries to shine some light on the "terrible" carbohydrates and debunk some popular myths. Most of the chapter consists of explanatory details of certain refined carbohydrates with the subtitle "Breaking Down Carbohydrates". The digestive process of carbohydrates starts in the mouth and with enzymes, like amylases, these chains of monosaccharides break down to glucose, the building blocks, and shorter chains, like sucrose and lactose.

Refined sweeteners are produced from artificial ingredients or natural sources, serve multiple purposes in food manufacturing, like adding sweetness, texture, and flavor, but are nutritionally void and mess up blood glucose and taste buds. Intact whole grains are often refined into flours (refined grains), which deprives them of the essential for nutrient absorption components of bran and germ. Products made from such flours are metabolized too quickly for the liver and pancreas to control blood glucose and deprive the bacteria participating in the digestive process of many nutrients. A combination of resulting factors creates insulin resistance. What whole carbohydrate-rich foods contain that make them nutritional are micronutrients, highly bioactive compounds that work as information blueprints for cells, and are analyzed next.

Vitamins assist in thousands of metabolic reactions, can be found in fruits, vegetables, and intact whole grains and are classified into fat-soluble vitamins and water-soluble vitamins. Minerals are nutrients that can't be generated by living organisms, but play a list of vital functions in the human body and can be found mostly on plants. Fiber is a nutrient that its behavior in the digestive track is still being explored. It is known, though, that fiber is mostly consumed by the bacteria composing our body, which makes beneficial short-chain fatty acids with it. Fiber also helps slow the rate of glucose absorption into the blood and move undigested food material through the intestine. Fiber supplements do not behave as such. The authors also label water as a micronutrient to underscore its role in the thousands of chemical reactions and the help it provides in the digestion and absorption of food. It can be found in whole foods and constitutes most of the mass of raw fruits and vegetables as displayed in a table. There are compounds that assist in the repair of damaged cells and extend their lives, called antioxidants. They are found in brightly colored plant foods in nearly 64 times bigger quantities than in animal foods. Lastly, plants exclusively contain phytochemicals, compounds that reduce the risk of premature death and are known to have various health benefits for many organ systems.

The rest of the chapter describes step-by-step the metabolizing process of carbohydrate energy. On step one intact whole carbohydrate chains enter the liver, slow the digestive process and limit glucose in the liver and on the blood. Refined carbohydrates create excess glucose and a minimal amount of that turns into fat through the DNL process. On the second step, this acceptable rate of glucose in the liver, allows its cells to produce ATP and distribute it around the body. It works like a command central with high demands for ATP and micronutrients. The third step points out that the liver also stores glucose in the form of large molecule tanks called glycogen to provide itself with energy and the brain with its most preferred fuel. The last step explains that muscles also store glucose as glycogen for later use. The more carbohydrate energy is consumed the larger the glycogen stores become.

Are you enjoying the book so far?

If so, please help us reach more readers by taking 30 seconds to write just a few words on Amazon.

Or, you can choose to leave one later...

Chapter 7

Chapter 7 has a self-explanatory title "The Ketogenic Diet vs. a Low-Fat Plant-Based Whole-Food Diet: A Comparison of Short-Term and Long-Term Results" and begins with the story of Patricia, who switched from a ketogenic diet to the Mastering Diabetes approach to achieve her desired goals. The authors start the chapter by stating some important concerns regarding the ketogenic diets before they acknowledge a serious amount of research studies about its beneficial short-term effects. Ketogenic diets were first used for their anticonvulsant effects, but when some other side effects like weight loss and flat-line blood glucose were noticed, doctors started directing it to patients with metabolic conditions. Studies from all over the world demonstrated its short-term effectiveness since the ketogenic diet was very widely used. However, in Korea researchers were the first to report on certain side effects they encountered. One notable exception to the short-term improvements was the LDL cholesterol; ketogenic diets actually raise it.

The next part of the chapter explores the long-term effects and is titled "Ketogenic Diets in the Long Term: A Less Positive Outlook". A great number of scientific studies are cited to draw attention to the consistent results of the long-term consumption of animal products. All the studies mentioned extend in a longer than a decade time frame and include tens of thousands of cases. Some studies and meta-analyses tried substituting proteins and calories from animal foods with those from plant foods resulting in a decrease in participants' risk for death from cardiovascular disease, cancer, or any cause. Some others had a wide variety of diets that people followed and concluded that those who ate more meat and dairy increased their risk for all-cause mortality and disease-specific causes. All studies were consistent with their findings; reducing consumption of animal foods reduces total mortality, and increased consumption of plant foods also reduces the risk. Those effects were amplified for people living with diabetes. A shift from an animal- to a plant-based ketogenic diet produces the same or even greater beneficial short-term effects - evident in short-term research – but there is no long-term research on the effects. Since that diet (called Eco-Atkins diet) requires high consumption of total fat, its side effects in the long run probably will coincide with the findings that are mentioned in the third chapter.

Since this diet greatly benefits people with diabetes, the authors accentuate that the total amount of insulin injected per day is not the most important metric of a person's diabetes health. A more valuable metric and a very strong indicator of the overall insulin sensitivity is the carbohydrate-to-insulin ratio. That ratio has a positive correlation with insulin sensitivity and a negative one with risk for chronic disease. Since all "diets" work in the short term and there isn't only one way to enjoy those beneficial effects, the authors strongly caution against ketogenic diets and advise adopting a diet that creates long-term sustainable habits and provide lasting metabolic fitness.

In the next part titled "Now for the Good News" the authors cite and describe a number of small scale short-term studies that occurred progressively over time starting from 1920 to very recently. The results were remarkably positive for low-fat plant-based whole-food diets and were repeated to the same effect later adding weight stability to rule it out as a factor for the counter-conventional results they produced within days. Even though there aren't any studies of truly low-fat plant-based whole-food diets in large numbers of people over long periods of time, there are studies that contextualize the effects of such diets.

The last part of the chapter explores the connection between "Heart Disease and a Low-Fat Plant-Based Whole-Food Diet". The risk of complications of diabetes is the main concern of people living with diabetes and heart disease is the leading cause of death. Diets high in fat, with the worst offender being saturated fat, accumulate arterial plaque which through a simple process results in a high-pressure hardened blood vessel that can eventually become fully occluded, resulting in a complete loss of blood flow. The only diet known to reverse heart disease is a low-fat plant-based whole-food diet supported by overwhelming scientific evidence that the authors present arraying a significant amount of recent studies.

Chapter 8

The core of the book is in the eighth chapter, the largest of them all, and is the introductory chapter to the Mastering Diabetes method titled "Getting Started with the Mastering Diabetes Method". As usual, it starts with a success story of this approach and then gives the first information about the method. The authors classify the participants according to their body reaction in the first 30 days of the program, specifically their blood glucose levels. According to their experience, 10-15% is the "slow responders", with a possible increase in their blood glucose levels, 10-15% is the "medium responders", with virtually no change on their blood glucose levels, and 70-80% is the "fast responders", with sudden reductions on their blood glucose levels. There are multiple genetic and lifestyle factors that affect the speed of response with exercise being the strongest. However, what the authors point out to be most important for their method to work is consistency.

The first and, according to the authors, one of the most important pieces of information in the book is that the A1c is an incomplete indicator of a person's diabetes health. I can easily be reduced by all kinds of diets, although diets high in nutrient density also yield significant protective effects against chronic diseases. The book offers some guidelines to the reader on how to set and achieve SMART goals about his diabetic condition.

Subsequently, the authors introduce in this next part of the chapter called "Your New Diet: Green Light, Yellow Light, and Red Light Foods" their new system summarized in a one-page table. According to them, green light foods can be eaten in abundance, are the most nutrient-dense foods, the least calorie-dense and with the highest water concentration. Yellow light foods are to be consumed in small quantities since they contain saturated fat and the goal is to minimize total fat. Some soy products are included in this category as well. Red light foods are completely excluded from the diet and they include two enormous categories: animal products and processed foods. Oil is also labeled red light food since it is 100% fat with no low nutrient density and contributes to insulin resistance. A similar system is adopted for beverages, too, with the same principals.

Furthermore, in the section titled "How Much Food Can You Eat?" five rules are stated and described to follow as guidelines. The first rules dictate "Don't Count Your Calories; Just Eat Until You're Satisfied" since green light foods are low in calorie density and high in fiber content, which speeds the feeling of satiation (feeling satisfied after a meal). Rule number 2 calls for attention in total fat consumption, offers a table for the appropriate maximum consumption of fat per day according to exercise levels. The third rule urges to "Remember That All Whole Foods Contain Carbohydrate, Protein, and Fat" and a variety of foods, even green light foods, may lead to unexpected consumption of fat, that combined with a small number of yellow light foods, will exceed the daily limit. Another table is provided for reference. The next rule encourages to "Treat Fruit Like Your New Best

Friend" and reminds the reader that only when consumed with high-fat foods pose a threat to blood glucose levels. The authors also provide a step-by-step strategy of increasing fruit intake. The fifth and last rule recommends creating the daily habit of logging the food carefully and honestly in nutrition logging software to ensure accurate depiction of daily calorie sources with little effort.

The following section is devoted to essential fatty acids (EFA). There are two EFAs that the human body can't manufacture: omega-3 and omega-6. Although both are essential to get from the diet, omega-6 should be more restricted. That is because, apart from the useful compounds it produces, persistent omega-6 pathway activation induces chronic inflammation and deprives omega-3 of the necessary enzymes it needs to produce anti-inflammatory compounds. The authors recommend keeping track of the omega-6 to omega-3 ratio every four months and adjusting the diet.

The last part of the eighth chapter discusses fat-soluble vitamins, which are essential for tissue function. Vitamin A is important among others for eye and teeth health, skin integrity, reproduction and can be found in red, orange, and yellow-colored fruits and vegetables. Vitamin D is connected to bone growth and remodeling and can be obtained from sun exposure and supplementation, though the optimal level is controversial. Vitamin E has antioxidant properties, works best combined with vitamin C, and can be easily obtained from green light foods. Vitamin K is essential for blood clotting and bone growth and can be obtained from leafy greens. Evidently, to maximize fat-soluble vitamin absorption there is a minimum daily amount of fat required. The authors point out the insufficiency of proper research for the exact amount of fat required, but they propose a low daily intake, easily achieved. Vitamin B12 is also mentioned, which is essential and water-soluble, and the authors recommend taking a supplement to include it in the diet. The chapter ends urging the reader to "Focus on the Big Picture" and offers resources on "How to Find a Plant-Based Doctor".

Chapter 9

The ninth chapter is titled "Getting to Know Your New Needs: Diagnostic Blood Tests and Managing Oral Medications" and does a deep dive in those medications educating the reader. The authors mention another astonishing success story of the Mastering Diabetes Method and suggest than any changes to lifestyle and medication regiment should only be made with a healthcare provider to be effective and safe. Subsequently, they refer to "Diagnostic Blood Tests" and provide the mnemonic PILAF to remember the five biomarkers that should be measured. Resources and a table with more information are provided. The c-peptide blood test is the first one mentioned which indicates how much insulin the beta cells are capable of making and it can determine the entire course of the diabetes treatment. The second blood test mentioned is the diabetes antibody panel which measures whether the immune system actively attacks beta cells or insulin. For both tests, ample information is given.

Afterward, the chapter discusses diabetes medication. The authors suggest monitoring the overall trend of blood glucose levels instead of micromanaging it and for insulin-dependent people calculating the new basal insulin needs and adjusting it within the first few days. They also describe a strategy to adjust bolus insulin in the first weeks of transitioning. They provide a tool called "Decision Tree" to track daily all the necessary variables that affect glucose metabolism. The goal is to gain a deep understanding of the person's own metabolism and even make accurate intuitive predictions about the need for injecting insulin for insulin-dependent people. They provide details, examples, and resources to make the whole process as convenient as possible.

"An Overview of Oral and Injectable Diabetes Medications" is the title of most of the rest of the chapter and aims to give an overall understanding of commonly prescribed diabetes medications. They are listed in order of their risk for causing hypoglycemia during the transition: bolus insulin, basal insulin, sulfonylureas, meglitinides, GLP-1 receptor agonists, DPP-4 inhibitor, SGLT-2 inhibitor, thiazolidinediones, alpha-glucosidase inhibitors, amylin analogues, and biguanides. In the end, the authors remind the readers again to have frequent communications with their doctor and that pharmaceutical medications are not designed to treat the underlying cause of chronic diseases, but changes in lifestyle do.

Chapter 10

Chapter ten is titled "Starting Strong: Breakfast" and aims to build the first meal of the day according to the Mastering Diabetes program. It begins with an incredible success story of one of the program's coaches. The book introduces the readers to an insulin resistance quiz and then classifies them into four categories according to their baseline insulin resistance. Then each category is assigned a certain "breakfast option" that is described next. The category with the lowest score is assigned the first breakfast option which includes many fruit servings and certain seeds. Every other category is assigned the second breakfast option which is rich in fibers to protect blood glucose, but eventually, all categories end up shifting to the first option. The authors give plenty of details on them and even suggest including medicinal plants, like amla, to their "perfect breakfast options".

The next part of the chapter is called "What About Gluten?" and discusses the effects of gluten intolerance in the digestive process. Although celiac disease is an autoimmune condition, the connection of beta-cell destruction and gluten intolerance is interesting and is now being researched. The gliadin fraction of gluten can trigger not only a series of reactions that lead to developing the celiac disease but also to another autoimmune reaction that might result in the destruction of beta cells. Most of the green light foods, like fruits and legumes, have protective effects against gluten. A simple experiment is described to determine the effects of gluten on the reader. Concerning caffeinated beverages, the authors suggest completely eliminating sodas and energy drinks, mostly because they are highly processed foods, however, caffeinated tea is allowed. Black coffee is allowed, but the preparation process is encouraged to retain its positive metabolic effects. Smoothies are also not encouraged because blending breaks the long-chain fiber molecules resulting in rapid glucose absorption and less food for the microbiome. The last part of the chapter offers some advice for occurring problems like blood glucose levels during the transition and ends by stating the requirements that if met, the participant can safely move on to changing his lunch.

Chapter 11

" "Gaining Momentum: Lunch" is the title of the eleventh chapter and serves the purpose of building the habit of eating the "perfect" lunch. Like every other chapter, it starts by recounting a success story of the Mastering Diabetes program and then states the importance of lunch as the middle-of-the-day meal before going into "The Ins and Outs of Calorie Density: A Lifestyle of Abundance". Calorie density is a term that refers to the number of calories in a given weight of food and the range is wide in commonly eaten foods. Even though there are yellow and red light foods low in calorie density, the authors don't recommend building the meal around them, since they have a great impact on insulin sensitivity. Green light foods are the least calorie dense foods and as long as a wide variety is consumed, they can be eaten in abundance. Research has shown that people eat approximately the same weight of food on a daily basis, therefore if there is a strategical consumption of green light foods, then there is little room for yellow light foods and none for red light foods resulting in a great calorie reduction.

In this section of the book "What Makes You Feel Full?" the authors discuss the complex communication system of the human digestive system and the brain which consists of a combination of hormones, like serotonin, neurons and short-chain fatty acids. They also mention bulk, a compound of water and fiber that occupies space in the digestive system and mechanically stretches the stomach sending the most effective satiety signal to the brain. Green light foods are rich in both fiber and water, which means that they contribute significantly to the bulk effect. Some comparisons of foods are presented to showcase both the difference in calorie density as well in nutritional value and satiation contribution.

Subsequently, the chapter focuses on how to "Construct the Perfect Lunch" by firstly giving ample information on constructing "no-recipe" meals that are easy, fast, satisfying and very energetic and even include dressings. Next, they analyze the benefits of batching cooking and preparation, which are saving money, ensuring constant food availability and making it easier to prepare healthy meals. Specifically, they suggest batching cutting fruits, cooking starchy vegetables, intact whole grains, legumes - whose preparation takes a lot of time -, cutting up non-starchy vegetables, cleaning green, cooking make-ahead meals, sauces, and condiments and storing them all in the fridge or freezer. The authors also give instructions on executing those batched tasks. They also suggest building the habit of planning the meals of the next 5-7 days, which will make easier the preparation, the shopping, and the "committing" part. They offer compelling tips and tricks on grocery shopping and inform that the total amount of food shopped will be increased, but the bill probably will decrease. Choosing organic products is almost always preferred, but packaged meals not so, because they usually contain artificial sweeteners. They urge readers to exercise more self-awareness than self-judgment when going grocery shopping.

Chapter 12

The twelfth chapter with the title "Developing a Routine: Dinner" discusses mostly how to protect the habit of having a healthy dinner. Another success story is mentioned and then some instructions on the "perfect" dinner. Usually, dinner is the largest meal of the day and although the authors recommend lighter meals at the end of the day, they also suggest building them around more calorie-dense green light foods like non-starchy vegetables and leafy greens. In order to protect this healthy meal from the effects of decision fatigue, the chapter accentuates the importance of batch prepping and having ready-to-consume most of the dinner ahead of time.

The rest of the chapter offers tactics and tips on protecting this important meal when "Eating at Restaurants and Cafés". Social events are a great threat to the Mastering Diabetes method, but there are some strategies that help to cope with them. "Strategy 1: Pre-Eat Your Dinner" has many advantages. Firstly, eating to almost satiation calorie-dense foods before leaving the house will make it easier to choose foods with green light ingredients and the hunger will be much more manageable. Since restaurants don't usually offer satisfyingly large portions of such foods, there won't be a need to buy more and it'll be easier to resist the pre-meal snacks that are often served. That is also the second strategy, to order only green light foods by choosing certain appropriate dishes and making small modifications. The key factors for success at eating at restaurants are planning and communication. Planning includes choosing ahead of time the place of visit; plant-friendly restaurants make the job much easier. Planning also includes choosing what to eat. The menu can work as a list of ingredients that are available to make custom and tasty meals; the authors give tips on locating everything. Communicating effectively and politely can help to dodge awkward situations. It's a good idea to talk to a server away from the table to explain the reasons for ordering custom plates and of course their content. Being polite, humorous and thankful always make it easier and the authors offer tips for all of that. Some of these techniques can also work when going at dinner parties, with some modifications; planning and communicating are sufficient. Social events might sometimes lead out of curiosity to interrogation. Some useful tricks are offered freely for this situation, too and the chapter closes with the requirements for the next part of the Mastering Diabetes program, fasting.

Chapter 13

Chapter 13 is titled "Intermittent Fasting for Increased Insulin Sensitivity and Weight Loss", illustrates the benefits of fasting, one of the cornerstones of the Mastering Diabetes Method and like every chapter starts with a success story to highlight its point. The authors argue that fasting is not as difficult as it seems, it may be ingrained in our genetic material from our human ancestors and be quite advantageous. Laboratory observations in animals and researches imply that calorie restriction results in slowing the aging rate, weight loss, improving cognitive health and preventing chronic inflammation conditions like cancer, heart disease, and diabetes. Negative calorie balance ensues intermittent fasting, which forces the liver and muscles to burn already stored fat and glycogen, increases insulin sensitivity and reduces the risk of cardiovascular disease.

The book mentions five fasting methods, but only focuses on two, the 16:8 daily intermittent fast method and the once-per-week 24-hour intermittent fast method, due to their sustainability. There are examples for both methods and tips for easing through the fasting period, like drinking fluids (water and green tea), being aware of the body cues and taking part in distracting exercises. The fasting period always starts immediately after a meal and includes sleeping hours, too. The book also proposes a modified once-per-week 24-hour intermittent fast method for specific, more vulnerable, people, because of the effects on both the physical and the emotional state – hungry and angry is a thing. Evidently, some snacks options are offered for the modified version. There also some advice for people who are underweight and wish to have the benefits of fasting. Discerning between two kinds of hunger, physiological and emotional, the authors propose understanding them and developing the ability to distinguish them. The chapter closes giving three prerequisites to move on the final step of the process, exercise.

The fourteenth chapter explains the effects of exercise on people living with diabetes and is titled "Exercising for Maximum Insulin Sensitivity". The authors tell the story of a competitive athlete with diabetes 1 who managed to run 40 half marathons in 12 months after switching to the Mastering Diabetes lifestyle. To illustrate why exercising is so beneficial a small part is dedicated to explaining "Mitochondria: The Powerhouses of the Cellular World" and their relationship with insulin resistance. Mitochondria live in every cell of the body in various densities and produce ATP, the fuel for thousands of reactions inside the cells. Each liver cell has thousands of mitochondria which are crucial for insulin secretion. Insulin resistance and mitochondrial dysfunction have a "chicken-and-egg" relationship. That means that one causes the other, insulin resistance imposes mitochondria on producing free radicals which in return cause extensive cell damage and insulin resistance. High-fat diets aggravate those effects, but exercise reverses them. Regular exercise for people living with diabetes acts as a substitute for insulin, reducing the amount of insulin necessary to control blood glucose levels.

Afterward, the authors teach how to incorporate regular exercise into a daily habit through a progressive five-step process. The first step requires identifying a specific goal, for example, to exercise for 3 hours per week. Starting small (30 minutes every day) makes consistency easier and when it comes to intensity the rule of thumb is "exercise at a pace that makes it challenging to talk to someone else or sing your favorite song." Step two is to define the preferred exercise. The authors give examples of cardiovascular, resistance and combinatory exercises and their health benefits. Key questions are mentioned to identify favorite exercises; music is suggested as a powerful motivator. The third step asks to capitalize on accountability by either finding a partner or joining a local gym/group that has regular meetings of the reader's favorite sport. The next step strongly suggests creating a schedule for the exercise routine and then putting it down somewhere visible. The fifth and final step instructs to start slow but consistently; frequency, duration and intensity will increase over time, there is no problem starting slow.

The next part is titled "Controlling Your Blood Glucose Before, During, and After Exercise". For insulin-dependent people, the book recommends raising the blood glucose before exercise giving ample instructions and for non-insulin-dependent people, the book states that there is no such need. Concerning eating before exercise, a diet rich in carbohydrates supplies the muscles and the whole body with sufficient energy and keeps the glycogen stores full. Eating some carbohydrate-rich foods 1-2 hours before exercising offer a slight boost of energy, but can't substitute a proper diet. Research has shown that adding nitrate-rich vegetables impacts profoundly the blood vessels. Specific advice is given to people using insulin pumps on how to control their blood glucose during exercise. In the case of hypoglycemia during exercise, the authors recommend eating 1 or 2 fruits and give detailed instructions on how to handle it. After exercising the body enters two phases of afterburn that are characterized by high insulin sensitivity that can last up to 72 hours later. The first 1-3 hours after exercise are the best window to nourish the body on carbohydrates and antioxidants. However, there is a specific emphasis on the potency of exercise compared to a low-fat plant-based whole-food diet, which is considerably lower. Finally, the chapter ends giving 5 "toolbox strategies" that, when practiced, indicate that the reader is optimizing his insulin sensitivity toolbox.

Chapter 14

The final chapter of the book titled "Meal Plans and Recipes" offers in great detail cooking methods, equipment, time-saving strategies and recipes which are in absolute agreement and an integral and essential part of the Mastering Diabetes Method. Some appendixes follow including information and promised examples of specific topics mentioned before.

Background Information about
The Mastering Diabetes

The "Mastering Diabetes: The Revolutionary Method to Reverse Insulin Resistance Permanently in Type 1, Type 1.5, Type 2, Prediabetes, and Gestational Diabetes" by Cyrus Khabatta Ph.D. and Robby Barbaro MPH, was published on February 2020 by Penguin Random House and became immediately a New York Times bestseller. It is based on the Mastering Diabetes program created by the authors, who have been living with type 1 diabetes for a combined total of 36 years. Their online coaching program has helped thousands of people to reverse type 2 diabetes and prediabetes, get exceptional blood glucose control in type 1 and 1.5 diabetes, achieve an excellent A1c, reach their ideal weight, lower their cholesterol, blood pressure, triglycerides, gain energy and live their lives on their terms. The book is heavily backed by evidence-based science, it cites more than 800 scientific references and contains numerous stories of people who successfully followed the Mastering Diabetes method and changed their lives. It explains all the science behind the low-fat plant-based whole-food diet and its connection to insulin resistance and blood glucose. This is a book not only for people living with diabetes or even some other chronic diseases but for anyone who wants to learn the effects of food in his body and wishes to create a healthy lifestyle.

Background Information about
Cyrus Khambatta, PHD & Robby Barbaro, MPH

Cyrus Khambatta was diagnosed with type 1 diabetes in 2012, his third autoimmune condition, and tried to control his blood glucose following his doctor's advice. Soon he found out that it wasn't working, he shifted to a plant-based diet and took the matter on his own hands. He now has consistently A1c value between 5.3-5.7%. He has a degree in mechanical engineering from Stanford University as well as a Ph.D. in nutritional biochemistry from UC Berkeley. He co-founded the Mastering Diabetes coaching program and has helped thousands of people.

Robby Barbaro was diagnosed with type 1 diabetes in 2000 and on his journey to health he experimented a lot and studied heavily. He tried all kinds of diets, but since he shifted to plant-based he has consistently A1c value between 5.3-5.7%. He has a master's degree in public health and spent six years helping build the Forks Over Knives empire. He co-founded the Mastering Diabetes coaching program and has helped thousands of people.

Trivia Questions about
Mastering Diabetes

1. What is the role of insulin in the body?

2. How is a high-fat diet inducing insulin resistance?

3. What is insulin sensitivity?

4. What is the role of glucose in the human body?

5. How is fiber beneficiary for the digestive system?

6. How are free radicals dangerous for the body?

7. What foods can be eaten in abundance?

8. Is A1c a sufficient indicator of your diabetes health?

9. Why is it important to log daily your food?

10. How is fasting contributing to insulin sensitivity?

11. How is exercise contributing to insulin sensitivity?

12. What is a decision tree?

Discussion Questions about *Mastering Diabetes*

1. Why is the low-fat plant-based whole-food diet not the standard diet for people with diabetes?

2. How is treating insulin resistance affecting other chronic diseases?

3. What is the most difficult part of transitioning to the Mastering Diabetes method?

4. Can the Mastering Diabetes lifestyle benefit people with no chronic diseases?

5. In what ways does society make it difficult to follow this lifestyle?

6. Which success story from the book is almost "too good to be true"?

Thank You!

Hope you've enjoyed your reading experience.

We here at Book Tigers will always strive to deliver to you the highest quality guides.

So I'd like to thank you for supporting us and reading until the very end.

Before you go, would you mind leaving us a review on Amazon?

It will mean a lot to us and support us in creating high-quality guides for you in the future.

Thanks once again and here's where you can leave a review.

Scan me

Warmly yours,

The Book Tigers Team

Download Your Free Gift

Before you go any further, why not pick up a free gift from me to you?

Natural Detox Strategies

Discover The Most Effective Detox Strategies For a Successful Cleanse.

Scan the barcode to get it before it expires!

Discover the Book Tigers Series

If you are enjoying reading our books, please take a moment and check our book series.

SELF HELP & SUCCES SUMMARIES

FICTION SUMMARIES

SOCIAL & POLITICS SUMMARIES

HEALTH & DIET SUMMARIES

Feel free to continue your journey with us, where you will find new resources, tools, blogs, and advance notice of new books at...

https://www.booktigers.com

Made in the USA
Middletown, DE
25 February 2022

61814599R00031